Uncle Ng
Comes to America

T0163276

Uncle Ng performing at the Asian American Arts Centre, late 1980s

Uncle Ng often performed at the annual folk art Lunar New Year festival with other performing artists, surrounded by exhibitions of Asian folk art and with fellow folk artists based in New York City.

Uncle Ng
Comes to America

Chinese Narrative Songs
of Immigration and Love

edited by
Bell Yung & Eleanor S. Yung

mccmcreations

Uncle Ng Comes to America

Published by MCCM Creations 2014
www.mccmcreations.com
info@mccmcreations.com

Editors & Translators	Bell Yung and Eleanor S. Yung
Project Director	Christopher Mattison

Papercuts and photo credits
Asian American Arts Centre, New York City, Frontis, preface, p 22, 24, 37, 56, 67
Robert Lee, p 8 / The Uncle Ng family, p 12, 18, 40, 59 / Cover photograph, Leh Chyun Lin, commissioned by the Asian American Arts Centre for the exhibition "Folk" Tradition, New York City, 1991

Supported by SOMA (Project on the Sustainability of Memory & Artifact)
City University of Hong Kong

TABLE OF CONTENTS

Uncle Ng in San Francisco, 1996

Uncle Ng was invited by the Chinese Culture Center of San Francisco
to perform at a special gala event in April 1996.

Preface

Bell Yung & Eleanor S. Yung

This multimedia publication brings together, for the first time, song texts, audio recordings, and a documentary video on muk'yu and the singer Uncle Ng. The song texts have been transcribed into written Chinese and translated into English. Two essays provide background material on the singer and the songs; the third reminisces on the hardships faced by early Chinese American immigrants.

Muk'yu 木魚 is a form of folksong sung widely throughout southern China in both rural and urban areas.[1] These songs are part of the everyday life of the common folk. Sung mainly for their own private enjoyment, muk'yu are rarely performed for a public audience, and hence have no monetary value. No recordings were known to exist, whether commercial or made by researchers in the field, before Uncle Ng made his own. However, muk'yu texts were widely published in cheaply printed booklets from at least the 18th century up until the mid-20th century. Sung throughout the Pearl River Delta, where the Yue language is spoken in its many diverse forms, the muk'yu of each region uses the local dialects and musical styles. The muk'yu collected in this volume are all sung in the Toisan (in Putonghua, Taishan 台山) dialect, which was the language spoken by a majority of the early Chinese Americans. The first generations of immigrants to North America were predominately from the Toisan region.

Ng Sheung Chi 伍尚熾, whom everyone called Uncle Ng, was born and lived in Toisan until he moved to New York City's Chinatown in 1979, at the age of 69, to join his family. Having grown up singing muk'yu from the time of his youth in a farming village, Uncle Ng continued to sing on the streets of New York. What was unusual about Uncle Ng was that he sang the songs whenever and wherever, produced homemade cassettes of his performances, and sold them to anyone who cared to listen along the streets of Chinatown. Indeed, with

---

[1] The two Chinese characters "muk" and "yu" literally mean "wood" and "fish." There are different theories about why this type of song is called "wooden fish," none of which is definitive. See Leung Pui Chee, "Muyushu di neirong yu liuchuan jiqi yanjiu di guoqu yu xianzai" 木魚書的內容與流傳及其研究的過去與現在 (The content and dissemination of muk'yu texts and its research, present and past). *Journal of Oriental Studies*, vol. 14, no. 1 (January 1976), 65–82.

his particular musical talent and love for the songs, he transformed private tales into a public testament of his own life history and those of his community back home. The most poignant works are the personal stories by Toisan's early immigrants to Gold Mountain (Jinshan 金山), the name given by these travelers to San Francisco specifically, and to North America as a whole. Uncle Ng brought these tales full circle back to the New World. Other muk'yu that Uncle Ng sang were of love and courtship, among which the best known is the saga "The Floral Writing Paper" (Huajianji 花箋記), also known as "The Eighth Scholar's Story" (Diba Caizishu 第八才子書),[2] which is one of the earliest pieces of Chinese literature to be translated and published in English. Although an extant version of the text of "The Floral Writing Paper" dates to the early 1700s, there are no known recordings of its performance before Uncle Ng's.

Uncle Ng was one of the last great folksingers. His superb musicianship was innate, having had no formal training. Yet he was more than a transmitter of ancient songs; he created new tales based on personal experience and his own brand of narrative and musical talent. As Uncle Ng says in the film *Singing to Remember*, he sang because it was how he remembered his past. When Uncle Ng recounted his own journey to the Gold Mountain in 1979, his story was in striking contrast to similar songs of earlier generations that he had learned back home. His own songs show how different the Gold Mountain is today from previous eras, yet he faced new challenges that the old immigrants never could have imagined. Performed with keen observation and heartfelt emotion, the song is not only Uncle Ng's personal voice, but the voice of millions of immigrants, from China and elsewhere, that landed on American shores. The song "Uncle Ng Comes to Gold Mountain" is a rare example in which a folksong creator's identity is known.

———

The Uncle Ng Project began more than 20 years ago in 1989, by the Asian American Arts Centre of New York.[3] The project consisted of several stages and components. The first step was the making of *Singing to Remember*, a 16-minute documentary of Uncle Ng that was completed in 1991. This video helped Uncle Ng win the prestigious National Heritage Fellowship from the National Endowment for the Arts in 1992. The film was screened at the Margaret Mead Festival, the Slice of Life Festival, the Los Angeles Asian Pacific

[2] K. C. Leung translated "Diba Caizishu" as "Eighth Work of Genius." See K. C. Leung, "Chinese Courtship: The Huajian Ji in English Translation," in *Chinoperl Papers* 20–22 (1997–1999), 269–288.

[3] The Asian American Arts Centre, founded in 1974 as a not-for-profit organization, promotes the preservation and creative vitality of Asian American cultural growth and its historical and aesthetic linkage to other communities, by presenting and interpreting the ongoing synthesis of contemporary American and Asian art forms, utilizing art exhibitions, new media, research and documentation, and public education. *http://www.artspiral.org/about.html*

Film Festival, the Through the Lens Festival, and was broadcast on WNET (NY), KCET (LA), and WYBE (Philadelphia).

Shortly after the completion of the documentary, the Arts Centre began recording Uncle Ng singing muk'yu. During the recording sessions he sometimes was accompanied by his daughter Soping Ng and their friend Teri Chan. The process took four years, during which time Uncle Ng recorded many of his favorite songs. Eight of these songs are included here. Some were selected because of their relevance to the Chinese American historical experience, others because they were favorites of Uncle Ng.

These eight songs were then transcribed into written Chinese, under the supervision of Uncle Ng himself. The Chinese texts were next translated into English, a collaborative effort by Joanna Lee, Sonia Ng, and Su Zheng. Uncle Ng was also consulted on the meaning of many Toisan words. The English translation of the song "Uncle Ng Comes to Gold Mountain" first appeared in *Artspiral*, a publication of the Asian American Arts Centre; Su Zheng later published an article on Uncle Ng and his songs.[4] The translation of all eight songs was further revised at different stages by Bell Yung, Andrew Miller, and David Rolston.[5]

Of the eight songs, "The Story of Gold Mountain" depicts the experience of a sojourner of an earlier age who traveled to America seeking a better life for himself and his family back in China. It narrates the survivals and hardships of Chinese laborers in the American Wild West during the gold rush days. "Nephew Goes to Gold Mountain" consists of two letters, the first from an uncle in China to his nephew in America admonishing him for not writing, and for not sending money home to the young man's wife. The second section is the nephew's response. These two brief letters vividly illustrate the sentiments of Chinese families torn apart in the days of early Chinese immigrants in America. "Uncle Ng Comes to Gold Mountain" reveals the difficulties and ironies of the Chinese American immigrant situation in the late 20th century, while "Fellowship Acceptance Song, Washington D.C." was created by Uncle Ng on the occasion of receiving the National Heritage Fellowship. He performed the song to an audience of public officials, closing with ". . . wishing everyone promotions and great wealth and fortune . . ." to great applause and amusement. The "Toisan Embroidery Song" is a love song that incorporates many Chinese metaphors, from luscious peonies to distinguished historical figures. "Master Liang's Yearning," "Swearing

[4] Su De San Zheng, "From Toisan to New York: Muk'yu Songs in Folk Tradition," in *Chinoperl Papers* No. 16 (1992–1993), 165–205.

[5] The long delay in publication, which took over 20 years from the making of the documentary to the present volume, is due mainly to the Toisan language of the songs, which has required special care in the transcription and translation of the text.

Their True Love," and "Testifying to the Past" are three chapters from the muk'yu classic "The Floral Writing Paper" (Huajianji). These three songs were Uncle Ng's personal favorites.

Since the time of the Cultural Revolution in the mid-1960s, and with recent technological advancements and shifting tastes in popular culture, the muk'yu form has been under threat of extinction. Extensive fieldwork still needs to be done in order to search out and record any muk'yu that might still be sung in remote corners of the region. The original material collected in this publication will be of great significance to studies of folklore, oral literature, music, and, in particular, to histories of early Chinese immigrants to America. Through the audio recording and documentary film, a voice is given to the words, and a face and a personality to the singer.

NOTE ON ROMANIZATION

Chinese names and terms are transcribed according to different pronunciations within the context of the narrative: Putonghua, Cantonese, and Toisanese.

ACKNOWLEDGMENTS

We are grateful to all the supporters of this project, especially to Uncle Ng's family, who has stood by the Arts Centre during the development of this project over the last 20 years. We are grateful to the following for grants awarded during the various stages of Uncle Ng's project, which is now culminating in this publication: the National Endowment for the Arts, the New York State Council on the Arts, the Lila Wallace Reader's Digest Fund, the Boulton Foundation, and the Research Grants Council of Hong Kong.

We also would like to acknowledge support from Brooks Williams of Harmonic Ranch in the recording and mastering of Uncle Ng's songs, Tony Heriza in the making of the documentary *Singing to Remember*, with usage of historical footage from Jon Alpert of Downtown Community Television, and Betty Lee Sung for her contributions.

We also would like to thank Wing Tek Lum, Jody Arnhold, Germaine Wong, Arthur Neis, and May Jew for their support, and Johnny Fu and Christine Lee for their assistance.

Last but not least, we want to thank all the supporters and friends of the Asian American Arts Centre over the years, and all those who have waited patiently (and impatiently) for the publication of *Uncle Ng Comes to America*.

B.Y.
E.S.Y.

Uncle Ng (far left) with friends at Columbus Park in New York City's Chinatown, 1992

Uncle Ng
Robert Lee

When I first met Mr. Ng (pronounced as *Eng*) Sheung Chi, he was singing in a community park in New York City's Chinatown for his own enjoyment, as much as for anyone else who might be listening. He was singing a form of folk song that I had never heard before. Some songs were zesty; others were gentle, even tender. Clearly he loved to sing, and he obviously wasn't bashful. He walked back and forth as he gestured, emphasizing lines with his hands and arms. A thin man with a ready smile, he dressed as seniors do, in many layers. As I got to know him and the world he opened up to me, I came to appreciate his kind, humorous, and heartwarming manner, as well as the joy he took in life; qualities I learned that were prized by the rural village culture from where he came.

Mr. Ng was known among his fellow senior citizens as Ng Bok 伍伯 (Uncle Ng). He often sang muk'yu with other Chinese American seniors, who also knew these songs, in the park and at the local senior center, or by himself on the streets of Chinatown. Sometimes people stopped to listen, but usually people simply ignored him and continued on with their busy lives. He was unperturbed; New York in the mid '80s was easy, a piece of cake. Uncle Ng could hardly stop himself from singing.

Uncle Ng was born in 1910, in Gampei 錦被 (known today as Gamfoon 錦歡), a small village in Toisan County, one of the main areas of immigration to the United States for more than 150 years. Today, the Toisan people still constitute one of the largest Chinese groups in America. Before Uncle Ng immigrated to the U.S. in 1979, he spent most of his years working in the fields as a farmer. He learned to sing muk'yu when he was only seven or eight years old by listening and imitating other villagers. At the age of eighteen, Uncle Ng was recognized as an outstanding singer of muk'yu by his fellow villagers. "When I sang, even the birds would fly down to listen to my singing." Later in life, he wrote out the text of the songs he knew to help expand his repertoire.

Uncle Ng recalled: "Singing was very popular; everyone sang. Villagers used to sing in the rice fields, or more often, after a full day of work, the whole village would gather under the shadow of a few large trees to get some fresh air and to enjoy singing. Two people might sing a duet, with each person taking turns singing alternate lines. A particular song might continue for hours. It was just folk singing for one another. Whenever we felt good, we sang a few lines. I sang whatever came to mind. Informal singing competitions might occur at weddings and at annual holiday events, or with nearby villages that were within walking distance on the other side of the fields."

According to Uncle Ng, the popularity of muk'yu declined precipitously due to the criticism initiated by the Cultural Revolution. He once told me a story about how his songs survived these changes. At regular cadre meetings, where thousands were gathered in a stadium, Uncle Ng's singing was so popular that he was expected to begin the meetings with a song. However, instead of the revolutionary songs that were generally required, he would sing a muk'yu love song.

Uncle Ng eventually made his way to America to join his children. His hope, like the waves of immigrants before him, was to become rich and return home. After arriving, he worked for several years in garment factories. After retiring, he continued to live with his wife and daughter. In addition to the traditional repertoire of love stories, Uncle Ng particularly favored those songs that recount the experiences of early Chinese immigrants. One of his original compositions vividly describes his own life, "Uncle Ng Comes to Gold Mountain." This story touches upon the difficulties and ironies of the Chinese American immigrant situation, of why Uncle Ng left China, of the conditions in Chinatown, and yes, of life everywhere. "There are many in this world who believe, / That when you have money and rice everything gets easier."

The pace and texts of such songs are intimately descriptive of the Toisan people's experiences and sensibility. Chinese Americans from this area can recall, as they listen to songs both delicate and strong, an era of calm enjoyment and pleasing pastimes. The sorrow they experienced arising from immigration to America also finds expression here. Suppressed emotions find freedom in these songs. This folk culture embraces without question that the whole of life is the heritage of Asian Americans. And it remains just below the surface, beneath the tumult of the street life that is Chinatown. For me, Uncle Ng's muk'yu singing reflects an aspect of the American historical experience and the very meaning of being Chinese in America.

In 1992, Uncle Ng was named a recipient of a National Heritage Fellowship, which recognizes master practitioners of a traditional art or craft who have made "valuable artistic contributions both to their local communities and to the country as a whole . . . The awards give vivid testimony to the creative genius of the many peoples who compose our nation." Uncle Ng was the first Chinese American to receive this award. During a U.S. Congressional reception, he met then President George H. W. Bush, and later performed at a gala public concert at Georgetown University to an audience that included nearly 700 Washington bureaucrats. He sang a traditional love song and one of his own creation for the occasion. His performance was enthusiastically received by a thunderous standing ovation. The audience's reaction took me by complete surprise, and it has since convinced me of the little known capacity of China's indigenous culture. At 82 years of age at the time, Uncle Ng was still a captivating performer, with his simplicity, direct nature, and charm.

The Asian American Arts Centre nominated Uncle Ng for the National Heritage award as a way to highlight the rural culture of the Toisan region. It was hoped that such an award would call the attention of Chinese Americans to the value of their indigenous heritage. Here was a man who could enable Chinese Americans to see beyond the limits of the Pacific Ocean, beyond the claims and stereotypes of elite culture. His songs could enable Chinese Americans to appreciate and understand the nature of their roots in a region such as Toisan, and to connect with a simpler way of life as an alternative to the fast pace of New York City. As demonstrated at the Georgetown University concert, other Americans were susceptible to an unassuming folk artist homegrown in China.

When the announcement of the National Heritage award came in the mail in 1992, we broke the news to Uncle Ng, explaining every detail carefully. He listened intently, thanked us profusely, and went home. The following week he stopped by for a visit, sauntering in even more relaxed than usual. He was wearing a white straw-like plastic hat, thin plaid minty green and white shirt over another plaid shirt, which was worn over a T-shirt, dark baggy pants, and his same old sneakers. He looked as though he had just won the lottery and was having no trouble knowing what to do with the money. His complexion had changed; he seemed somehow more satisfied, even though he had always been jovial and gracious. He was clearly happy and we were very proud of him.

The local Chinese newspapers covered the story, some with full-page articles. Four years later, in 1996, the Chinese Culture Center of San Francisco invited Uncle Ng for a concert performance of muk'yu; he was warmly welcomed and given a grand reception.

Since Uncle Ng's passing October 7, 2002, at the age of 92, the broader question of muk'yu as a dying art form remains. Yet there are signs of hope, such as the American-born singer Charlie Chin, who has shown in his music a distinct similarity to Uncle Ng. Having studied with a Toisan storytelling master, the late Leong Chi Ming, Charlie's American folk songs exude the same zest and tenderness as Uncle Ng—tales both amicable and strong. Wisdom brewed with the meaning of life rises from his music. Thus, transformed and in a new context, cultural forms are reborn.

Uncle Ng and Family, 1946

From left: Uncle Ng's second oldest daughter, wife, oldest son,
mother holding his third oldest son, Uncle Ng holding his second
oldest son, and eldest daughter. The woman in the back row is
Uncle Ng's youngest sister.

Muk'yu: Voices of the People
Bell Yung

Muk'yu narratives are widely sung in Southern China in communities around the Pearl River Delta. Based on a poetic text and a simple traditional melody, muk'yu tell stories long and short; some weave complicated accounts from China's long history, legends, and folk tales; others are personal, topical, adulatory, or lyrical. They all generally express deep personal feelings. While most other forms of story-singing are performed mainly by professional singers for a paying audience, muk'yu are sung by ordinary people for their own enjoyment: men and women, at work or at leisure, singing mainly to and for themselves, or along with friends. These songs are performed and appreciated for their own sake rather than for any commercial or ritualistic purpose and can be thought of as the true grassroots voices of the people.

Muk'yu compositions vary in length from dozens of lines to extended stories with thousands of lines that might take tens of hours to sing.[1] The verse structure tends to be highly uniform: a string of lines each of which has seven syllables. With very few exceptions, the lines form couplets, triplets, or quadruplets that are defined by the linguistic tones of the final syllables of each line. For a long song, the lines are grouped into chapters; within a chapter, the lines may be further grouped into sections based upon subplots of the story. These sections are marked by end rhymes: all the lines within a section would have their ending syllables follow the same rhyme, while a subsequent section shifts to a different rhyme for the ending syllables.

Musically, muk'yu repertoire within a particular regional style share a simple short tune, which is sung repeatedly to a couplet, triplet, or quadruplet of text for all the textual units throughout the song, and for all the songs in the repertoire. In some regional styles, a singer may use the same melody throughout a song, or may move to a different tune to begin a new section or chapter of text. However, the shape of the melody is quite fluid: the details of the melodic twists and turns within a song are quite flexible so that, when comparing one unit of text to another, the "same" tune may sound somewhat differently among the units. The only rigidly unchanging component is the final pitch of a line and the melodic formula that is associated with the final pitch.

Muk'yu is almost always sung without instrumental accompaniment, which allows the singer to burst into

---

[1] For detailed discussion on the textual and musical structure of muk'yu, see Su de san Zheng, "From Toison to New York: Muk'yu Songs in Folk Tradition," Chinoperl Papers No. 16 (1992–1993), 167–205.

song at any time and during whatever activities. Rhythmically it can be quite free, with a vague sense of beat, but otherwise following natural speech rhythms.

In a larger context, the songs are considered part of the narrative tradition found throughout China. Known as *quyi* 曲藝, literally "song-art," or *shuochang* 說唱, "speaking-singing," the origin of the Chinese narrative tradition can be traced back to religious chanting by Buddhist monks in the Tang dynasty (7th to 10th century) over a millennium ago.[2] By the 10th century, the songs had evolved into a form of secular and commercialized popular entertainment. Throughout the centuries a great variety of regional forms and styles were developed. The narrative song tradition has for centuries served two major social functions: as popular entertainment in the pre-technological age and as a form of mass education. Before the 20th century, the vast majority of Chinese people were illiterate or semi-literate; narrative songs offered them a view of the wider world, and played a major role in affording the Chinese people a shared sense of history, myths, and mores with which to forge a cultural identity.

Muk'yu songs have a large number of regional styles that differ in linguistic and musical characteristics. Southern China around the Pearl River Delta is densely populated; however, the hilly terrain and the many waterways have served as boundaries that help to preserve the regional linguistic and cultural characteristics among pockets of villages and townships. Muk'yu narratives, which flourish throughout this area, are sung in the regional languages and dialects, many of which are unintelligible from one another. The linguistic differences affected musical characteristics, so that muk'yu from the Toisan area, where Uncle Ng was from, sounds different from muk'yu in Canton (Guangzhou 廣州), Yanping (Enping 恩平), and other areas. When Uncle Ng came to New York City, he found many compatriots from Toisan who spoke his language and who greatly appreciated his singing.

One sign of the popularity of muk'yu is evidenced by the large number of crudely-printed booklets of muk'yu texts (Muyushu 木魚書) for mass consumption, which were widely circulated in the Pearl River Delta from at least the early 18th century.[3] For example, the song "Huajianji" (The Floral Writing Paper), included in this publication, has an extant text dating to 1713. It is among the earliest works of Chinese literature to be translated and published in English, in 1824. The translation was carried out by the Englishman Peter Perring Thoms, who gave it the title "Chinese Courtship in Verse." The

---

[2] For a general discussion of Cantonese narrative songs, see Bell Yung, "Cantonese Narrative Songs," an entry in the China Section, *Garland Encyclopedia of World Music Vol. 6: East and Inner Asia*, ed. Robert Provine, Tokumaru Yoshihiko, J. Lawrence Witzleben. 2001.

[3] On muk'yu booklets, see Sonia Ng, Guangfuhua shuochangben muyushu di yanjiu 廣府話說唱本木魚書的研究 "A Study of the Cantonese muk'yu songbooks," Ph.D. dissertation, The Chinese University of Hong Kong, 1989.

work also reputedly impressed Goethe.[4]

One may ask: if most muk'yu singers and listeners were illiterate, why were these booklets printed? One reason is that the booklets served as a tool for singers to teach themselves to read by following a written script of a text that they already knew by having learned it orally. A singer gradually learned to recognize certain recurring written characters and, with some help here and there from a friend, became literate. Another well-documented function of these booklets was for fortune telling: a vender would display a stack of booklets for a customer to randomly pick one. Using the title of the booklet that was chosen as a starting point, the vendor-fortune teller offered advice as well as the booklet for sale. This was an effective way to distribute the muk'yu booklets.

Beginning from the middle of the 20th century, the spread of newer forms of mass entertainment such as radio, film, and later cassette recorders, compact discs, television, and video discs gradually replaced the singing of muk'yu; consequently the texts were no longer printed. But even as late as the 1970s, one could still run across old copies of muk'yu texts in used bookstores. As the texts disappeared, so did the muk'yu singers. By the end of the 20th century, only very few elderly singers, such as Uncle Ng, could be found.

Among the songs in this collection, "The Floral Writing Paper" is representative of the many longer songs that weave complicated stories from China's rich heritage of folktales. Three chapters of the multi-chaptered text are included in this volume (Tracks 5, 6, 7). "Toisan Embroidery Song" (Track 4) belongs to a category of short, lyrical songs without narrative content. The song is constructed of a string of auspicious names of flora and fauna. Based on its content, this song was most likely sung as part of the wedding ritual.

The other five songs are particularly poignant from the American perspective. Uncle Ng came from the county of Toisan, which has a long history of sending young men to work in North America, known as Gold Mountain. Naturally, a repertoire of muk'yu developed around the experience of the early migrants. Through a poetic text and a simple tune, these songs express the anxiety, longing, and hardship of both the sojourners and their families back in China. Particularly moving is "The Story of Gold Mountain" (Track 2) which tells the story of a mineworker in the New World thousands of miles from home. In vivid detail, the song is a valuable record of the trials and tribulations of several generations of overseas Chinese laborers in the United States. "Nephew Goes to Gold Mountain" (Track 3) has similar content, but in the form of two letters exchanged

---

[4] For discussion of the textual versions of "Huajianji," see Leung Pui-chee (Liang Peichi), Ed., Huajianji: Huijiao Huiping Ben 花箋記：會校會評本 (The Story of the Floral Writing Paper: Edited and Annotated). On a discussion of Thoms's English version, see K. C. Leung, "Chinese Courtship: The Huajian Ji in English Translation," in Chinoperl Papers 20–22 (1997–1999), 269–288.

between a nephew who went to the Gold Mountain and his uncle who remained at home. These songs must have been widely sung in the Toisan area at the time when Uncle Ng was growing up, as similar kinds of songs are found in old muk'yu booklets. We are fortunate that Uncle Ng sang them in America; thanks to the Asian American Arts Centre, they were preserved in recordings for posterity, for it is unlikely that anyone still sings such songs back in Toisan today.

An interesting contrast to these songs of early immigrants is "Uncle Ng Comes to Gold Mountain" (Track 1) and "Fellowship Acceptance Song, Washington D.C." (Track 8). These two songs are unusual not only because they are original creations by Uncle Ng, but because they reflect upon experiences of new Chinese immigrants in America at the end of the 20th century. The "Fellowship Acceptance Song" in particular struck a personal and optimistic note about the hope and joy of a new life far from home.

To understand more fully the artistic structure of muk'yu, consider the song "Uncle Ng Comes to Golden Mountain" as being illustrative of the textual and musical characteristics previously mentioned. The song is relatively short with only 57 lines, some of which form couplets. Theoretically, the couplet structure adheres to the verse structure of classical poetry in which the upper and lower line of each couplet is defined by the linguistic tone of the final word of each line: the upper line should end in an oblique tone, and the lower line in an even tone. However, Uncle Ng treats this rule rather flexibly.

Instead of alternating between oblique and even tones to form couplets, he sometimes allows two or three lines to end in the same tone category. Such flexibility also affects the tune, since melodic features are determined to a considerable extent by the tone categories of the individual syllables of the text.

In general, each line has seven syllables (zi, or written characters) with an internal structure of 2+2+3. However, for most of the lines, Uncle Ng adds a number of "padding zi" to increase or even double the total number of syllables in each line. This is common practice in muk'yu, as well as in other types of narrative songs, and testifies to the improvisatory nature of the genre.

With very few exceptions, all the lines rhyme within a section. According to the rhyme scheme, the 57 lines may be divided into the following categories. Note that a new rhyme is introduced when the text initiates a new idea.

lines 1–5, -iang rhyme
lines 6–11, -ong rhyme
lines12–15, -iang rhyme
lines 16–22, -ong rhyme
lines 23–26, -ei rhyme
lines 27–33, -ai rhyme
lines 34–54, -ong rhyme
lines 55–57, -in rhyme

Musically, the entire text is sung to one basic tune. Beginning from line 37, Uncle Ng shifts to a lower pitch, though retaining the same tune. Was this a conscious artistic decision to indicate a different musical mood, or was Uncle Ng simply tired and decided to use a lower pitch to ease his voice? With Uncle Ng's passing, and as the singing of muk'yu gradually disappear throughout the Pearl River Delta, we may never know the answer. There are very few recordings of muk'yu in any of the variants of the Yue language, which makes the work presented in this volume of even greater value. It is also a testament to Uncle Ng's extraordinary musicianship and the significance of the muk'yu narrative tradition for future generations.

Uncle Ng's Passport Photo, 1979

History as Reflected in Song
Betty Lee Sung

For the early Chinese immigrants who came to America to open up and develop a new nation, life was more than rough. It was downright brutal. Many of them emigrated out of poverty. They had been farmers, but the land could no longer feed them or their families. Some bound themselves into eight years of indentured servitude simply to gain passage to America. Others were kidnapped and sold into bondage because of the huge demand for labor in the West. Most, however, came through the credit-ticket system whereby they mortgaged their labor for a steamship ticket.

The trip from southern China to California by boat was no bargain either. The men did not have a cabin or bed assigned to them for the three-month journey. They were herded into the ship's hold like cattle with little air or light, and then thrown and tossed about when waves rocked the vessels. Finally reaching land, they would come ashore, only to be locked up in prison-like detention centers, such as Angel Island, where they were interrogated until immigration inspectors determined whether they would be admitted. That was post-1882, after Congress had passed the Chinese Exclusion Act, which denied all persons with Chinese blood the right to enter the United States, except for those who could claim citizenship through birth or parentage, who were one of the five exempt classes, or who had re-entry permits.

Chinese immigrants endured all of these indignities because of the high expectations and illusion of wealth; a belief that the new land was a mountain of gold where one could pick up nuggets and become rich overnight. Gaining entry to the United States meant coming to Gold Mountain, a synonym for the U.S. that has endured to this day.

Hard work was not the only burden that they had to endure. Chinese immigrants were used to hard work. Theirs was the muscle that brought forth gold from the bowels of the earth to enrich this new found land. After gold, it was the silver mines, and then the crops they grew to feed the masses swarming westward. Then to tie the continent together, it was necessary to build a transcontinental railroad. The Chinese became the primary labor force of the Central Pacific, laying tracks over the mountains and across the deserts that gave the eastern seaboard access to the West and vice versa. The Chinese were praised for their industry and their accomplishments, but when the railroad was completed, they were laid off and condemned for providing competition to white labor when they sought other jobs.

Hounded, harassed, chased out, persecuted, discriminated against, murdered, massacred, their homes burned, denied employment or even a place to live, the Chinese huddled into Chinatowns for safety and protection. In Walla Walla, Washington, they were jammed onto a train, hauled to the end of the line, dumped out into sub-freezing temperatures, and left to perish. In Tacoma, Washington, all of the Chinese in town were herded onto a ship to be sent back to China. The ship was so heavy it could not move. In 1885, twenty-eight Chinese were massacred in Rock Springs, Wyoming. Chinese laundries were burned and when the occupants tried to escape, they were shot or left to die in the flaming buildings.

The Chinese began to disperse to other regions from the West. Wherever they went they could generally only find jobs as domestics, farm laborers, or else they began small enterprises such as hand laundries, grocery stores, or restaurants. At that time the Chinese population was almost all male, a so-called bachelor society. This meant no feminine companionship, no warmth of family, no children to ease the burden of a day's hard work. The laundries, restaurants, and groceries were generally scattered throughout a city to avoid competition, so fellow countrymen were not nearby to exchange pleasantries or to chat. Life was isolated and lonely, from dawn to dusk.

Chinese women were absent from the early days of Chinese American history. Recruiters wanted only men for the backbreaking labor, and Confucian culture prescribed that the men, though married, had to leave behind a wife to care for elderly parents. In addition, U.S. immigration laws made it difficult for women to enter the country after 1882. The few women who did venture west prior to the exclusion were suspected of immorality and denied entry. On top of that, the Page Act of 1875, decreed that any woman with American citizenship would lose that citizenship if she married an alien. This deterred American women from marrying anyone Chinese, and miscegenation laws forbade interracial marriages.

In this way the Chinese men were condemned by racial identity, through no fault of their own, to a life of loneliness. They could not go back to China to visit because they might not be allowed back into the U.S., unless they had papers showing that they had derivative citizenship or were from one of the exempt classes. Even when they had these documents, they were detained again at Angel Island, or a similar detention center, upon their return, sometimes for weeks or months, merely because they had a Chinese face. Is it any wonder that those men who were literate composed verses that mirrored their experiences, pouring out their souls?! Some of the lines were carved on the walls of Angel Island and others were set to song following the muk'yu pattern of syllables and rhyme. As someone brought up among these early immigrants in the 1930s and 1940s, and seeing the hard lives they led, I know many wrote verses lamenting the shattered hopes and dreams of being in this country and of the harsh lives they led.

Life for the Chinese in the United States did not change until after World War II. The Exclusion Laws finally were repealed in 1943, but until 1965 only 105 persons of Chinese blood were allowed to enter the United States in accordance with the immigration laws. Women did not appear in any real numbers until the War Brides Act that permitted all men who served in the armed forces to bring their wives to America. Not until the Immigration Act of 1965, which did away with the national origin quotas and enlarged the country quotas, did Asians start moving to the U.S. in any real numbers. Today, Asian Americans are one of the fastest growing minority groups. The 1940 U.S. census lists 77,504 Chinese. As of 2010, the Chinese population in the U.S. stood at almost three and a half million.[1]

Memory is short, and it is hard to envision what life was like just a few decades ago except as it is recalled in muk'yu, which may become a lost art. Uncle Ng came to this country after the Cultural Revolution in China, a period when muk'yu songs were forbidden. Fortunately, Uncle Ng's passion for the songs that he learned as a boy enabled him to recall and to express his repertoire, sharing the tales in Columbus Park in New York's Chinatown.

[1] http://www.vasummit2011.org/docs/research/The%20 Vietnamese%20Population%202010_July%202.2011.pdf, last accessed 12/30/2011.

SONG TEXTS

伍伯來金山   Uncle Ng Comes to Gold Mountain

清閑無事多思想	In idle moments my thoughts pile up,
想起木魚我就唱	When I think of muk'yu I begin to sing.
該片木魚非別樣	These muk'yu all
又來回憶我家鄉	Recall my hometown.
一言難說事又長	Hard to put into words, the story is long,
四十年前得解放	Forty years ago my hometown was liberated,
一朝天子一朝王	Each court brings a new emperor.
乜樣事情唔唱我唔講	Some events I will never sing or talk about,
勞勞苦苦築水塘	Toiling hard we built reservoirs.
水利過關生產禾苗壯	Water increased production and the seedlings were strong,
糧食豐富蒔芋谷米滿糧倉	Produce was plentiful, sweet potatoes and rice filled the granaries.
世間幾多人咁思想	There are many in this world who believe,
有錢有米好商量	That when you have money and rice everything gets easier.
兩條路線各方向	Of the two political lines that moved in opposite directions,
誰人唔望出外洋	Who wouldn't want to go overseas?
夜又想　日又望	By night I thought, by day I planned,
辦乜條件出香港	To find a way to get to Hong Kong,
猶如凡夫上天堂	Like a mortal striving for heaven.
到香港　舉頭望	Arriving in Hong Kong, I raised my head to admire,
高樓大廈真威煌	The skyscrapers and apartment buildings so truly impressive.
人逢喜事精神爽	When you reach a happy event your spirit soars,
想著金山條路走忙忙	Mind fixed on the road to Gold Mountain I hurried along.
人講美國就係天堂地	People say that America is a paradise,
個個發財又富貴	Where everyone becomes rich and lives the high life.
若然到達目的地	If I could reach my destination,
時開運轉發財亦未遲	My luck might change and I would become rich.

街上幾多人華麗
著起西裝打領呔
高雅靴子來行街
我亦只估到來美國嘆世界
誰知幾十歲人艱苦亦要捱
日食兩餐無時候
夜來寄宿住在康寧大廈十二層樓
日日閒遊隨街蕩
生活條件唔敢講
因為亞伯又冇銀紙入銀行
紐約街頭真興旺
交通便利人來多往
高樓大廈多工廠
過街要看紅綠燈
綠火唔著未好過街行
早起下床婦女番工廠
男人企檯兼做廚房
個個禮拜出糧銀紙冇處放
開個戶口存入銀行
餐館茶樓滿街巷
燈火輝煌做到天光
亞伯荷包冇錢唔駛講
荷包有錢一日飲幾趟
若有機會番到我台山四九五十錦被
金山客人來歸真威煌
村中兄弟來接兼來望
兄弟相逢真係爽

On the streets so many people were dressed glamorously,
Wearing western suits, neckties,
And stylish boots, they strolled through the streets.
I thought that once in America I would simply enjoy life,
Who would have thought that at my age I would still endure
such hardships?
Only two meals a day and at irregular hours,
By night I sleep on the twelfth floor of Hong Ning "Mansion"
Wandering idly on the streets each day,
I dare not tell others about my state,
This old man does not have a penny in the bank.
The streets of New York are thriving,
Traffic is smooth, crowds come and go,
There are tall buildings, apartments and many factories.
When crossing the street, you need to watch the traffic lights,
Do not cross the street before they turn green.
Rising early women go to work in the factories,
Men work as waiters and cooks.
Paid every week they have nowhere to keep their money,
So they open accounts and deposit wages in banks.
Restaurants and teahouses fill the streets and alleys,
They stay brightly lit until daybreak,
But this old man's wallet is empty, it goes without saying.
And if there were money in my wallet I would go drink tea
several times a day,
If there were a chance I would return to Toisan, to my village
Gampei, in the forty-ninth commune, fiftieth district,
How impressive I would be returning from Gold Mountain.
Brothers from my village would come and greet me,
Meeting them again would be wonderful.

今時不比往
派完銀紙又派麻糖
兄弟談情講不盡
又來回家見親人

Things would not be as they were in the past,
I would distribute money and then sesame candies.
We brothers would talk and talk without end,
And then I would go home to my family.

金山論 / The Story of Gold Mountain

請君莫講風流事	Let us not speak of romantic affairs,
又來說及金山人	But instead of people on Gold Mountain.
想壞條腸求大慾	They twisted themselves in knots figuring how to fulfill desires,
千計萬策必要來	Devising thousands of schemes to make their way.
唔學猶蠻個太子	It was not to imitate barbarian princes,
總係財神動我心	But instead the god of wealth that stirred my heart.
生得財來銀幾百	I borrowed a few hundred ounces of silver,
幾多利息不須言	How much interest I had to promise I won't even say.
心中自思和自想	In my mind I thought over and over,
一水船寄就還回	How it would be a quick trip over the ocean and back.
即時拋別宗和祖	I said my goodbyes to ancestors and clansmen,
又別老親及妻奴	As well as my elderly parents and wife.
幾處廟堂作落福	I visited several temples to pray and make offerings,
許落牌扁及金豬	Promising that I would donate plaques and offer roast pigs.
拆字先生都話好	Those who tell fortunes by analyzing characters all said good things,
算命先生又話靈	Those that tell fortunes by time of birth also predicted good luck.
村中幾多人讚羨	So many in the village praised or were envious of me,
亦有多人冷眼窺	But there were also many who looked upon me with cold eyes.
族中親朋都囑話	All of my relatives and friends urged me,
係好世情付回音	If the situation abroad was good to write them.
父母囑言唔去罷	My father and mother exhorted me to forget about going,
榮生外國好掛心	How they would worry about me living in a foreign country even if I flourished.
一兩黃金千兩福	"An ounce of gold is won in exchange for a thousand happinesses,
能得黃金不若然	Even if you get the gold it is not worth it."

妻子面前歡幾番
就將本業作生涯
紅杏碧桃難妄想
湖海飄遙幾月行
富貴貧窮天注定
聖人說話富難求
命裡有時終須有
命裡無時莫強求
父母高堂年老邁
供奉之人倚向誰
又有男細和女嫩
家務紛紛有主張
不若在家求別業
朝見父母晚見妻兒
一心想著富豪業
說盡千言有耳聽
睇見人人財滿足
講話艱難我不信
幾多人民都有利
豈獨我門不發財
到來一年和半載
三毫五百就還回
即時將我行李整
約齊同伴就登程
一怕半海銀被劫
二怕做民拐騙人
三怕大洋暈浪苦
四怕糧草不週全

My wife stood before me and tried to convince me,
Wanting me to stick with my current occupation.
 "I do not vainly crave apricots or peaches beyond reach,
For you to float across the ocean will take many months.
Wealth or poverty is determined by heaven,
The sages have said that riches are not easy to seek.
If you are fated to have riches then riches you shall have,
If you are not fated to have them then don't forcibly seek them.
Your father and mother are both very old,
Who will you rely on to care for them?
You also have young sons and tender daughters,
Household matters are endless and who will oversee them?
Is it not better to remain at home and find another kind of work?
Morning and evening you will be able to see your parents, wife
        and children."
My whole heart was intent on getting rich and honored,
Even pleading a thousand times I would have had no ear to listen.
I knew household after household who had become rich,
Even though they said it had not been easy I did not believe.
So many people had made their fortunes,
How could it be only my family that was not rich?
Within a year or so of arriving,
I would make a few hundred and then return home.
I immediately packed my luggage,
Having put together a group of fellow travelers we embarked.
Our first fear was we would be robbed at sea,
Our second fear was our papers had been prepared by swindlers.
Our third fear was the great waves would make us seasick,
Our fourth fear was our provisions would not last.

落在船中受盡幾多勞共苦	Stuck on that boat we suffered so much hardship,
大埠埋頭略歡心	Arriving at the wharf of the Great City was a relief.
共請馬車來入坑	Together we hired horse-drawn carts to the mines,
下車一望亦心煩	And what we saw getting out of the carts startled us.
屋在布帳床在地	For houses just tents and for beds just the ground,
石頭為枕草為床	Pillows of stone and beds of hay.
風霜雨雪任飄離	Wind, frost, rain, and snow blew over us at will,
樹木山頭形寂寞	The very trees and mountaintops looked lonely.
牛羊犬豬滿山放	Cattle, sheep, dogs, and pigs ran wild in the hills,
言語侏㑦番鬼樣	People spoke in strange tongues and looked like ghosts.
散髮披頭左衽妝	Their hair loose and unkempt, their clothes fastened on the left,
種類唔同我鄉黨	Their race different from that of my fellow villagers,
狼心惡毒驚猖狂	With hearts as evil and poisonous as wolves their savagery was startling.
禽獸野物時來往	Wild beasts and birds came and went as they pleased,
仲有山人驚我狂	Among them the mountain people terrified me.
舉目擔頭坑中望	Standing in the mine I raised my eyes to look around,
溶溶爛爛沙石光	There was nothing but wet sand and stone.
各處尋求心浪蕩	I sought here and there, my mind greatly unsettled,
擔起金漕悽惶惶	With my gold-panning tools on my shoulder, I felt lost and fearful.
一日尋求一二分	An entire day might bring only one or two hundredth's weight of gold,
日日空過不為奇	To go day after day finding nothing was not uncommon.
求得一圓心歡喜	If I found so much as a dollar's worth my heart was overjoyed,
又防醜鬼到來爭	But then I would have to guard against ugly ghosts snatching it away.
一尺土皮都要買	Even if only a foot wide I had to buy some land,
如若不買就閒遊	If I didn't buy land I would only wander aimlessly.
從此用銀來買得	So I started using my money to buy land,

又防醜鬼另霸佔
佢話搶時就係搶
佢話佔時就係佔
若有半句言微逆
即時打罵不饒情
今日往東明往西
尋金唔著甚艱捱
亦有鄉里人付好
大多拍手摸空囊
彼話走來真無用
使我來南亦是空
亦有到來三五月
一時勝彩就旋唐
此乃萬人無一個
一言百說甚英雄
亦有放懷和蕩子
洋煙賭吹及娼寮
亦有看見艱捱日
賣了糧田轉家行
重有人民千百萬
落在坑中甚艱難
水坑溶爛難入手
旱坑無水重難求
衣服破時靴又爛

But then I had to guard against ugly ghosts taking it by force.
When they said they would snatch it snatch it they would,
When they said they would claim it claim it they did.
If I uttered half a word ever so slightly against them,
They would immediately beat me and curse without mercy.
Today I go to the east but tomorrow the west,
Searching for gold but not finding it was hard to bear.
Although fellow villagers from home might have a bit of luck,
The majority of us clapped our hands and felt our empty pockets.
Some said coming here had been worthless,
I tried going south but that was also in vain.
Some came for only a handful of months,
Struck it rich and immediately went back to China.
But among ten thousand men I never found such an example.
One such story would be repeated hundreds of times, he would
          become heroic.
There were also those who let themselves go, good for nothings,
Who smoked, gambled, and went to brothels.
There were also those who found the life too hard to endure,
Sold their land and returned home.
But still tens of thousands of us stayed on,
Stuck in the mines in extreme hardship.
Mines flooded and it was hard to do anything with them,
Dry mines without water were hard to find.
My clothes were torn and my boots fell apart,

件件愛買又冇銀	Each of these I wanted to buy but had no money.
連嚟幾日無米飯	For several days I had no rice to eat,
借落黃金又冇還	The gold that I borrowed I was unable to repay.
春寒多冷人受苦	Cold in the spring and freezing in the winter I suffered,
風雨飄涼在坑邊	Wind and rain blew into the mines.
霜厚幾寸排水面	Many inches of ice floated on the water,
雪排幾寸滿山林	Many inches of snow piled up and covered the mountains and forests.
衣服床鋪如水濕	My clothes and bedding were soaked as if in water,
一層布帳外遮身	Nothing but a cloth tent to cover me.
又怕禽獸來吞噬	There was also the fear that wild beasts would gobble me up,
又怕野人射弓箭	Plus the fear that the wild natives would shoot me with arrows.
大石岩岩多險難	Great rocks piled on one another, the terrain was treacherous,
齊齊舉步又添愁	Though we trekked together we were still anxious.
夷狄橫行可患大	When the barbarians let themselves go trouble was great,
奪人圯口搶金銀	They would snatch others' mines and rob their money.
日間路途欄截剝	During the day they would ambush and strip us on the road,
夜間成群劫布帳	At night they came in groups to raid our tents.
大賊過江同一樣	The bandits who crossed the river were no different,
打死人命當平常	Killing people was nothing to them.
日日又愁身惡抵	Day after day we feared that we would not survive such abuse,
狼心惡毒甚行時	For they had the hearts of wolves, evil and poisonous when riled.
一到面前火打鑬	When they arrived they came with torches,
四塊銀紙就要來	Demanding even the smallest amount of money.
開聲驚懼言慄慄	From the beginning their voices were threatening and made us shudder,
半時一刻不饒情	They would not leave us alone.
倘或一時未照應	If we were a little slow in our response,
打罵橫行淚濕衣	They would beat us and curse, our tears would drench our clothes.
打打果然唔在講	Of course being beaten was not the worst,

重要銀子佢正行　　　　　What truly hurt was the money they demanded before leaving.
或有空囊噴夜冷　　　　　If our bags were empty we would be spat on in the cold night air,
割鬢剪髮不敢爭　　　　　If they cut off our hair we dared not protest.
但有鄉里來報上　　　　　If a fellow villager would come and report trouble,
走入你坑避一時　　　　　He would ask to hide in my pit for a while.
身在陰渠頭撲地　　　　　We would hide ourselves in the dark, heads pressed to the ground,
肚里將信又將疑　　　　　Our minds not sure if the bandits were coming.
如鼠見貓快快避　　　　　Like mice fleeing from cats we hid ourselves,
如鳥怕鷹立亂飛　　　　　Like birds afraid of eagles we scattered and fled.
若然俾佢看見你　　　　　If they saw you,
拿來削骨又剝皮　　　　　They would snatch you up, carve your bones, and peel your skin.
重有兄弟和鄉里　　　　　Other clansmen and fellow villagers,
唔敢行埋講平宜　　　　　Were afraid to approach and plead for mercy.
受盡幾多淒涼事　　　　　I put up with so many bitter and sorrowful things,
擔悶含愁冇心機　　　　　Dispirited and depressed I lost my drive.
前日想頭減大半　　　　　One day my hopes dashed I kept thinking over and over again,
棲身唔緊古悲漓　　　　　A place to stay was not the main problem, as sad as that was,
借落人家銀幾百　　　　　But that I have borrowed several hundred silver dollars.
摸下空囊心亦愁　　　　　Feeling my pockets empty I grew truly depressed. My mind sad.
賣田賠得乾淨淨　　　　　The money I received from selling my land at home is now gone,
縱然行得苦連連　　　　　Even if I can continue on, my life will remain hard.
鬼仔浚人真受欺　　　　　The foreign ghosts undermine us and I suffer their abuse,
無金可採又皺眉　　　　　No gold do I find which is more cause for worry.
幾多計較砌唔住　　　　　So many plans have I thought up without end,

如今想起恨差遲　　　　　　But now it is too late for regrets.
當初只話窮根斷　　　　　　Back then I thought only of cutting the roots of my family's poverty,
誰知今日債滿身　　　　　　Who would have thought that now I would be covered in debt?
日裡愁時行不樂　　　　　　Depressed all day I cannot find any pleasure,
夜間心煩睡不安　　　　　　At night my worries keep me from sleep.
一便行時一便嘆　　　　　　I sigh with every step I take,
一便食時一便愁　　　　　　I fret with every bite I swallow.
又愁無銀寄家裡　　　　　　I worry that I have no money to send home,
又愁家中債難還　　　　　　And my family at home cannot repay my debt.
愁得多來嘆聲出　　　　　　My sorrow is so heavy that I sigh out loud,
前世唔修受災磨　　　　　　What did I do in a previous life to suffer so much?
幾時愁到旋家日　　　　　　How much more sorrow before the day I return home?
歸家唐山講繁華　　　　　　When can I return to China and talk of prosperity?

侄往金山 — Nephew Goes to Gold Mountain

（一）叔去信 — (I) LETTER FROM UNCLE TO NEPHEW

<table>
<tr><td>

侄往金山只為家貧
今時運轉錢銀在身
許多快樂忘卻前恩
數你醜態逐一剖陳

衣裳奇樣綢緞衫身
三群五堆倒弄美人
四方城外攻打煙塵
登上樓閣絃唱是真
高朋滿坐酒肉為親
橫床玉枕吹笛如神
到處遊覽鞋襪常新
風流到此恰似洞賓
想你家吓淚流滿巾
結髮妻子饑餓誰憐
輪門乞食瓶生灰塵

床前啼哭眼起紅筋
我侄見字速付銀信
財帛到屋調解家人
勿為虛言至謹至謹

</td><td>

My nephew you went to Gold Mountain as your family was poor,
Now your luck has changed and you have money in your pocket.
In the midst of so much happiness you've forgotten its source,
Now let me recount your disgraceful actions, dissect them one by one.
Your clothes are outlandish and satin covers your body,
In groups of threes and fives you fool around with beautiful women.
When not playing mahjong you patronize opium dens,
In the brothels you take the songs for real.
In a roomful of patrons where you share wine and meat, you mistake them as friends,
Sprawled across the bed over jade pillows the flute sounds divine.
You travel wherever you like and your shoes and socks are always new,
In your leisure you are just like the trickster immortal Lü Dongbin.
When I think of your current life my tears soak my handerchief,
The woman you married when you both were young is starving but who takes pity on her?
From door to door she goes begging while the vessels at home are covered with dust,
By her bed she cries till her eyes are red.
My nephew, seeing these words, make haste to send money and news,
When this money arrives your family will be comforted.
Do not take what I say as mere empty words but sincere as can be.

</td></tr>
</table>

（二）侄來信

我來金山係為家貧
時時運滯無銀在身
許多苦楚受盡艱辛
估我在此享福做人
把我淒涼逐一剖陳
衣裳千補屎泡淋身
三白五削無處安身
天朦做黑難求黃金
火食不足那有餚晨
金山腳下大多窮人
如今在此恰似流民
幾日無食飢餓難忍
又想家嚇哭流滿巾
結髮妻子饑餓誰憐
叔台見字望念家親
亦為英雄在此景
金山改作困山名

(2) LETTER FROM NEPHEW TO UNCLE

I came to Gold Mountain because my family is poor,
Again and again my luck remains bad and I have no money.
In the midst of so much bitterness and suffering I experience only hardship,
You think that over here I am enjoying great fortune.
Let me take my misfortunes and lay them out to you one by one,
My clothes have a thousand patches, my body is soaked in diarrhea.
Completely impoverished, I have no place to stay,
From dawn till dark gold is hard to come by.
I do not have enough to eat so where would delicacies come from?
In Gold Mountain the majority of the people are poor.
In this place I am an outcast,
For several days I have not eaten and my hunger is hard to bear.
When I think of my situation my tears drench my handkerchief,
The woman I married when we both were young is starving but who
    takes pity on her?
Uncle, when you read these words I hope that you will think of my family.
The "hero" in this situation,
Gold Mountain should be renamed "Hardship Mountain."

台山綉花歌
（又名　娘子綉花歌）

列位齊坐下，
恭喜娘子你綉花，
紅線綠線綉成畫，
零時綉出幾繁華。
綉成水面開蓮花，
寶鴨穿蓮真清雅，
綉出盤桃唔係假，
綉成牡丹果無瑕。
綉隻黃鶯穿樹下，
綉個蝙鼠穿雲霞，
綉個將軍騎白馬，
綉個獅子靈銀牙。
綉個獅子石面，
綉條金龍駛出海，
孔雀開屏朝陽開，
白鶴穿雲天上來。
娘子真係手巧，
樣樣綉到好，
桃紅柳綠真秀貌，
金鳳錦輝現雲濤。
娘子真精通，
綉條鯉魚變成龍，
百花堂煌多出眾，
女子精通果係玲瓏。
娘子真係才情高，
綉出關羽帶二嫂，

Toisan Embroidery Song
(*or* My Lady Embroiders)

Everyone please sit down,
To congratulate my lady who embroiders so well.
You use red and green threads to create pictures;
In no time at all you produce images of affluence and prosperity.
The lotus blossom floating on water;
And around the lotus beautiful mandarin ducks elegantly glide.
The plate of peaches looks so real,
And the peonies are indeed flawless.
An oriole flies under a tree,
A bat dashes high above the clouds.
A general rides his white horse,
A lion bares his silvery teeth.
Here sits a stone statue in the form of a lion,
There goes a golden dragon diving out to sea.
A peacock displaying its magnificent plumage like the morning sun,
A white crane through the mist descends from heaven.
My lady, what dexterous fingers you have!
Everything you make is grand.
The red peach blossoms and green willow leaves appear delicate,
The golden phoenix gleams amidst the rolling clouds.
My lady, what craftsmanship you possess!
You can turn a carp into a dragon.
A hundred magnificent flowers outshining the others,
Your womanly skill is indeed exquisite.
My lady, you are so bright and talented,
General Guanyu guiding his sister-in-law.

張良許楮行計道，
繡個馬騮偷仙桃。
娘子真本事，
會繡又會做，
繡個武松打老虎，
繡成拐李駛葫蘆。

Zhang Liang and Xu Chu strategizing in battle,
The monkey steals the heavenly peaches.
My lady, you are so masterful,
You embroider well in addition to all else.
You produce a Wu Song who kills the tiger,
And the one-legged Immortal Li who carries his gourd.

Uncle Ng Singing at the New York Senior Citizen Center

Uncle Ng performed regularly at the Senior Citizen Centre,
especially during monthly birthday parties.

第八才子書：花箋記
(選輯三章)

The Eighth Scholar's Story: The Floral Writing Paper
(*Three chapters*)

（一） 梁生癡想

自送佳人歸去急
只見柳梢斜月映羅裳
疏星幾點明河漢
恨采園花弄晚香
那堪對此淒涼景
懶步回窗路見長
記得早間同弟講
佢話花前月下勿悲傷
于今撞著冤家債
不由人不斷肝腸
安排手段做個偷香客
花前就死亦何妨
歸窗一夜何曾睡
心心懸念此嬌娘
燈下見佢真美貌
俏麗唔同俗女妝
只帶青蘭花一朵
黑紗裙襯白羅裳
衫亦不長方到膝
玉指敲棋幾在行

(1) MASTER LIANG'S YEARNING

I bid farewell to my fair lady who hastily returns to her chamber,
With moonbeams reflected on her dress under the willow bough.
Under scattered stars and a bright Milky Way,
In sorrow I pick flowers in the garden, infused with the evening's
    fragrance.
Who can endure such desolate surroundings?
As I reluctantly stride back to my study along an endless path,
I recall speaking earlier today with my friend,
He asked me, among flowers and under the moon, not to be sad
But I met my love by fate as if a debt repaid,
I could not help but be heartbroken.
If only I could find a way to secretly make love to her,
I would not regret dying right there.
After returning to my study, I am sleepless all night,
I cannot stop thinking of my lady.
I imagine her so lovely under the lamp,
Exquisite, unlike the common women.
Adorning her hair with a lone green orchid,
She wears a black satin skirt with a white robe,
The robe just long enough to reach her knees.
She raises her jade-like fingers to lift chess pieces, playing
    with finesse.

莫道小生心事愴
料應泥佛亦思量
北便玄衣人亦好
私情只愛白衣娘
花間一見如膠漆
恨難飛入傍紅妝
忽聽雷聲頻入耳
月沉星落彩雲光

So please do not blame me for being so ardently in love,
For even a clay statue of Buddha would be charmed by her.
People in the north prefer women in black,
But I am attracted to my lady in white.
Ever since glimpsing her among the flowers I cannot bear
    to tear myself away.
I wish I could fly into her chamber and be by her side.
A sudden clap of thunder wakes me,
The moon has sunk, the stars faded, colored clouds glow.

（二）　誓表真情

慢講深閨情與意
又道梁生憶玉顏
光陰易過人難會
轉眼韶光八月間
多情一去無蹤跡
音書誰為寄嬌顏
算來今晚中秋節
家家弦管亂吹彈
對月幾多人快活
獨我多愁多恨積如山
金樽不落愁人肚
為娘事事盡丟閑
試問姮娥如有恨
光明何苦到人間
側耳城頭敲二鼓

(2) SWEARING THEIR TRUE LOVE

Let us stop here on the subject of the lady's feelings and desires,
And return to the story of Master Liang and a longing for his love.
Time passes easily but finding again his love is difficult,
For in a flash it is already the eighth month of the year.
The object of my desire has left without a trace;
Who will forward my love letters to my beautiful lady?
Reckoning by the calendar, tonight is the Mid-Autumn Festival.
Every family makes happy music with strings and pipes.
So many people enjoy themselves while they admire the moon;
Only I have nothing but sorrow and regret piled high as a mountain.
Good wine would not settle well in the stomach of this sad person.
Because of my longing for her, I have set aside all my duties.
If the moon-goddess herself is said to be sorrowful,
Why does she continue to shine brightly on mankind?
I hear the night watch from the city wall announce the second hour.

寒燈一點照愁顏　　　　　Only a cold lamp sheds dim light on my dreary face.
翠被生寒難獨臥　　　　　My green blanket is too cold to sleep under alone.
舉步遲遲出畫欄　　　　　I walk out wearily past the carved banisters,
竹徑無人風自響　　　　　No one else is there to listen to the wind along the bamboo path;
蓮池有月水生瀾　　　　　Only the ripples on the lotus pond reflect the moon.
忽聽誰家吹玉笛　　　　　Suddenly I hear someone playing the jade flute;
分明一調滿關山　　　　　It is clearly the tune "Deserted Mountains along the Western Border,"
吹起離人愁與恨　　　　　Which depicts the sadness and regrets of those taking leave.
兩行淚珠濕衣衫　　　　　As two streams of tears flow down and wet my clothes,
轉入橫門遊咽便　　　　　I turn to the side gate, heading another way.
月中流麗似人行　　　　　In the moonlight someone appears to be approaching.
走入柳陰忙躲避　　　　　I quickly move into the willow's shade, trying to hide,
睇見一群仙女降凡間　　　For I see some heavenly maidens descending to earth.
風舞羅衣飄旖旎　　　　　Their clothes, catching the wind, ruffle entrancingly;
嬌聲傳送到花間　　　　　Their charming voices can be heard among the flowers.
睇真又係楊家女　　　　　Taking a closer look, I recognize my lady from the Yang family,
瑤仙小姐共丫環　　　　　Lady Yaoxian and her two maids.
主婢三人遊月下　　　　　Together, the lady and maids stroll by, taking delight under the moon.
佢話一年好景有幾番　　　The lady says, "How many times a year do we enjoy such a sight?
雖然賞罷堂前月　　　　　Although we have admired the moonlight from the front parlour,
唔及得月明風景又遊行　　It does not match strolling among the scenery under the bright moon.
豈知人在垂楊下　　　　　She does not know that there is a man hiding in the shade of the
　　　　　　　　　　　　　willow trees,
許多情緒為嬌顏　　　　　Who is struck by her beauty and who has deep feelings for her.
走出花陰來作揖　　　　　He emerges from the shade and greets her with a bow:
姐呀有緣今夜慰平生　　　"My lady, we are destined tonight to meet, a special blessing on me."
碧月聞言將語道　　　　　Her maid Clear Moon upon hearing this asks,

誰人深夜到花間
小姐到來當躲避
膽大如天敢咁蠻
生聽罷　答言陳
伏乞妝台恕學生
一自棋邊相會姐
不辭路遠到跟尋
孤窗守盡淒涼夜
為娘操盡幾多心
今夜姮娥偏有意
團圓光照百花林
共姐細談風月事
庶唔辜負月中人
小姐細言公子聽
花間唔係武陵津
裙釵不管風和月
單曉深閨做指針
請君移步歸書館
隔牆花柳莫關心
梁生帶愧回言答
姐亦何須鐵石心
小生為姐長年病
相思無藥可除根
對月有時雙淚落
花前腸斷幾多匀

"Who is here in the garden so late at night?
When my lady comes, you should know better and take your leave.
How dare you be so arrogant, as if you have been sent from heaven."
Hearing her accusation, the young man explains,
"Please pardon this ignorant youth, prostrate in front of my lady.
Since I first met you at the chess game,
I have searched for you far and wide.
I have spent wretched nights staring out the desolate window,
And exhausted myself thinking of you.
Tonight the moon-goddess provided the opportunity
For us to be re-united under the moonlight amid a hundred
　　flowering bushes.
I want to speak with you in depth about the wind and the moon,
So as not to disappoint the moon-goddess and show our gratefulness."
The lady replies softly, "Dear sir, please listen to me.
This garden is not Wulingjin;
We ladies do not care about the wind and the moon.
We only know how to remain in our private chambers and practice
　　needlework.
Sir, please return to your study,
And please do not think more of the flowers and willows beyond
　　the study wall."
Liang, embarrassed by her response, says,
"My lady, why is your heart made of iron and stone?
For I have been ill all year due to my longing for you,
There is no medicine to cure my lovesickness:
Seeing the moon, two streams of tears often fall,
And my heart breaks many times before the flowers.

一身骨肉成消瘦
徬徨無主向誰人
面顏好似林間竹
改變形容有十分
日裡淒涼猶自好
第一夜深孤冷實難禁
極怕鼓聲催落雲頭月
破人肝膽碎人心
口固一陣傷情真惡抵
淒涼對實一盞斷腸燈
姐呀若然不信相思苦
試睇羅衣多少淚珠痕
姐若不瞅和不睬
分明對面喪殘生
我亦不敢怨娘虧誤我
偷彈十指怨前生
瑤仙亦見多淒慘
芸香難忍淚沾衿
行前叫句賢嬌姐
梁生果實見心傷
姐今不肯留心佢
恰如仗劍殺其人
我想女貌郎才真惡得
伯牙何處覓知音
願娘俯聽奴奴語

I have wasted away, am nothing left but skin and bone;
Feeling lost, whom can I turn to?
My face is as green as bamboo in the woods,
My appearance has changed completely.
During the day I can barely survive the sorrow,
And at night I can hardly endure the cold and loneliness;
Fearful that the night watchman's drumbeats may induce the moon
      to drop from the clouds,
They shatter my spirit and break my heart.
Waves of melancholy are truly hard to bear,
With grief and desolation I face the single lonely lamp, itself
      appearing heartbroken.
My lady, if you do not believe the anguish of lovesickness,
Just look at the lapels of my clothes and you'll see the teardrops.
If you insist on pretending not to see and ignoring me,
It will be the end of my destitute life.
I dare not complain that you owe me anything.
I can only reckon the sad fate that must have carried from my
      previous life."
Yaoxian is pained and moved upon seeing him and hearing his speech,
While the maid Incense Fragrance cannot help but shed tears upon
      her dress.
She comes forward and says,
"My lady, Master Liang is indeed heartbroken.
If you continue to ignore him,
It will be as if you pierced him with a sword.
I believe that a beautiful lady with a talented man is hard to come by;
Where else can Bo Ya find someone who truly appreciates his music?
Please listen to the words of your maid, my lady:

同郎發誓表真心
二家堅意無更改
做一段奇緣播世人
一來百歲諧連理
二則梁郎免掛心
自古鍾情非獨姐
何恨憐香惜玉人
瑤仙聽罷無言語
默對姮娥想未真
伶俐芸香知主意
叫言碧月過花陰
看雲亭上排香案
兩人移步到亭心
瑤仙羞對梁生語
妾長蘭閨十六春
垂簾未肯觀春色
花落花開懶去行
只知母訓勤針指
未曾移步出東鄰
今著為君垂愛我
花間無奈順郎心
但知夜誓同諧老
唔係淫奔喪節人
百年事在今宵定
一言為準不容更

Swear your love to the gentleman, reveal your true feelings,
That the two of you may pledge your firm commitment with no regret,
That your wondrous union will be for the whole world to know.
On the one hand, the two of you will be united for one hundred years
    to come,
On the other, Master Liang will no longer be anxious.
Since ancient times, falling in love has been something that everyone
    experiences.
Why make someone who cares for you regret his love?"
Yaoxian is silent upon hearing this;
She stares at the moon, unable to make up her mind.
The clever Incense Fragrance understands what her lady is pondering,
And asks Clear Moon to come with her beyond the shade of the
    blossoms,
To arrange incense sticks on a table in the Cloudview Pavilion,
And the young couple then walk slowly into it.
Yaoxian shyly says to Master Liang,
"I have lived in the seclusion of my chamber through sixteen Springs;
My bamboo blinds are always down; I did not want to view the beauty
    of spring,
Caring not about the blooming and wilting of blossoms.
I only listen to the advice of my mother and practice needlework,
And have not stepped beyond the eastern walls.
Now because you love me so ardently,
Among these blossoms I feel compelled to accede to your wishes.
I know only that our vow tonight is forever,
I am not one of those immoral women who behave casually.
Our union which will last one hundred years will be decided tonight;
Our vows will be irrevocable."

梁生帶笑回言答
感娘情義海般深
姮娥月府為憑証
誰敢忘情起別心
歷盡幾多愁苦處
事非容易到於今
袖中取出花箋紙
此紙將來寫誓文
你我各人收 紙
留為他日表真心
梁生舉筆琴台上
誓章同寫告知神
上寫二家名與姓
再寫芸香婢二人
事因姚府燈前會
問跡尋蹤到上林
百計千般才得見面
天緣有份遇著花陰
趁此月圓同發誓
一輪冰鑑照終身
男若負盟刀下死
永墮豐都不轉輪
女如背誓江中喪
難逃刀斧殺其身
寫畢二人齊下拜
名香三灶稟知神
一炷名香是馬牙
願郎文采筆生花

With a smile, Liang replies,
"I am moved by your love, which is as deep as the ocean;
I ask the moon-goddess to be our witness.
I shall never change my mind and shall be forever faithful,
Having experienced so much pain and sorrow,
I have not found my quest easy up till now.
I take out two flowery parchments from inside my sleeve,
To be used to write our vows.
You and I will each keep one,
Which will be proof of our true love for days to come."
Thus in the pavilion Liang writes on these sheets,
Writing the words of their vow to inform the gods.
At the top, he writes both of their names,
Then the names of the lady's two maids.
He continues by recounting the story: "We met for the first time
    at the Yao family's lantern festival,
Then I followed you to where you lived.
After trying thousands of ways to meet you I finally managed,
Thanks to heaven's fate, I have seen you again amidst the flowers.
Taking advantage of the full moon as we declare our love,
The luminous icy disk will shine on us to the end of our lives.
If the man breaks his vow, he will be slain by a sword
And never be reincarnated, but forever languish in hell.
If the woman breaks her vow, she will drown in the river,
Or die beneath an ax or cleaver."
After he finishes writing the text, both of them kneel down;
They pray to the gods and light three sticks of fine incense.
"The first stick is made of maya incense
To further the man's literary talent so that he shall pen flowery verse.

春風得意揚名姓
團圓衣錦早還家
香添二炷是黃擅
奴奴綠鬢對紅顏
早遂今生連理樹
芳名留取播人間
三炷沉香拜月神
百年惟願守初心
山盟海誓休辜負
地久天長學古人
拜告已完同步起
花前坐下細談論
梁生啟齒開言道
姐呀相逢記得係初春
今日夏完秋又到
正係守得雲開月一輪
咁久相思虧我捱
人話別離一日當三春
今晚相逢好似天邊月
光明長照世間人
我將姐比姮娥女
乞把團圓照學生
瑤仙羞愧回言道
誰人肯學卓文君

That his career will blossom, his name will be honored,
And return home in great splendor for our reunion.
The second stick is of yellow sandalwood
To bless our youth and beauty;
So that we can soon be together like two trees sharing the same roots,
And our fine story will be remembered by future generations.
With the third stick, made of chenxiang wood, we pray to the moon
    goddess,
That our love will last for a hundred years and remain the same as
    our first meeting.
The mountains and oceans are witnesses to our oath,
Our love will last as long as earth and heaven exist, to cite the ancients."
After these vows, they both rise;
They sit side by side in front of the flowerbed and share an intimate
    conversation.
Liang begins by saying,
"My lady, remember that we first met in early spring,
Now summer is over, and autumn is again here.
I have waited patiently for the dark clouds to pass and the moon to
    appear.
I have endured lovesickness for a long time,
People say that when lovers part for a day, a day seems like three years;
Tonight our re-union is like the perfect moon at the edge of the sky,
Whose radiance shines forever upon humans.
I compare you to the moon-goddess,
And beg you, like the moon, to shine on me forever."
Yaoxian shyly replies,
"Who would want to follow the example of Zhuo Wenjun?

奴本清廉窗下女
留心要學古賢人
今夜同郎花下誓
舉頭應愧月中神
只為東君頻著想
丟抛黃卷共青燈
恐怕為奴誤了終身事
故此順情盟誓啓郎心
若然逼我風花事
寧拾殘軀謝古人
免得東君長掛念
為奴丟冷讀書心
梁生見姐言推卻
花前飛淚灑羅衫
低頭不語長嗟嘆
一番憔悴把言陳
誰想玉容擔誤我
虧了高堂白髮親
料知別姐難長久
這回一定死歸陰
小姐見生情慘切
勸郎寧耐且歡心
到底有緣終配合
何苦花前迫結親
奴奴豈不知人苦
道理唔通勢惡行

I am but an innocent girl who has led a simple life,
Trying my best to study, learn and behave in accordance with the ancient sages.
As I vow my love to you tonight under the blossoms,
I feel ashamed to face the moon-goddess,
For I am afraid that if you spend all of your energy on our love,
You will abandon your books and your reading lamp.
Then you will have abandoned your career because of me.
That is why I took the oath in order to put your mind at ease.
However, if you force me into the affairs of wind and flower,
I would rather kill myself in honor of the ancient sages.
Then you would not go on longing for me,
And you would not sacrifice your studies because of me."
Recognizing her refusal,
Liang, amidst the flowers, weeps and sheds copious tears that soak his gown.
Lowering his head, he is silent, then heaves a deep sigh,
Crestfallen, he explains wearily,
"Who expects that your beauty will affect my career?
That I will then disappoint my elderly parents?
But I know that were I to part from you, I would not live much longer.
I am sure to die and head for the underworld."
The lady, upon seeing Liang's intense misery,
Comforts him and says, "Please remain hopeful and keep up your spirits.
If we are destined for one another, we will be together at the end;
But please do not force me among the flowers now.
Of course I understand your pain;
But I will not accede to conduct that is improper.

自小極嫌淫賤女
無媒苟合敗人倫
殺身誓不從郎命
堅心留待洞房春
梁生見姐無從順
只著含愁伴姐坐花陰
兩家談笑如膠漆
不覺城頭鼓五更
丫環催姐歸香閣
驚起離人兩淚淋
叫一句姐時心哽咽
此愁比舊又添新
閨中望姐留心事
莫將誓約當微塵
消息便傳鴻雁寄
免使寒窗寂寞盼娘音
瑤仙一發難分手
淚花浮粉把言陳
妾長朱門生繡閣
唔信相思會壞人
今日別君歸去也
始知離恨海般深
致囑功名須著意
早憑紅葉見雙親
相牽相扯難離別
無奈雞啼鳥噪月沉西
梁生步送瑤仙轉
四條銀淚亂交侵

I have hated licentious women from the time I was small;
A union without a matchmaker violates the moral code.
I would rather die than bow to your wishes,
I insist that we wait until our wedding night."
Seeing that his lady will not give in,
Liang can only sit sadly by her side among the flowers;
The two talk and laugh as if glued to one,
Not realizing that it is dawn, as signaled by the drums on the city
    wall striking five.
The maids urge the lady to return to her chamber;
Startled, the two lovers weep as they part.
Calling out "my lady," his heart breaks,
"This sorrow renews my old sorrow.
I hope that when you return to your chamber, you will think of me;
Do not treat our vows as if they were nothing but dust.
Please send me news by the wild geese,
So that I will not wait long in the loneliness of my chilly study."
Yaoxian also finds it difficult to say farewell,
Her tears wash away the rouge from her cheeks as she speaks,
"I was born into a rich family and grew up in a secluded chamber;
I do not believe that lovesickness can kill a person.
Today as I take leave of my lover and depart for home,
I begin to understand the grief of parting is as deep as the ocean.
Please work hard for the imperial examination, fame and fortune,
And return to see my parents with your title and honor."
Holding on to one another they find it difficult to part,
But the rooster crows, birds chatter, and the moon sets in the west.
Liang walks with Yaoxian to see her off,
With tears streaming down from both pairs of eyes,

一個耽愁歸綉閣　　　　One returns to her chamber in sorrow,
一個遲遲入柳陰　　　　The other walks slowly towards the willow shade.
好似鴛鴦遭浪湧　　　　Like two mandarin ducks struck by a cruel wave,
淒惶無主兩邊行　　　　They walk in different directions, both anguished, confused, and lost.

（三）　表訴情由　　　　(3) TESTIFYING TO THE PAST

生舉目　細觀親　　　　Liang raises his eyes, looks closely;
抬頭看見姐嬌身　　　　Lifting his head, he sees her delicate figure.
白米挪開將妹撒　　　　He throws a handful of rice at her,
妹罷妹叫一句瑤仙好斷魂　　And cries "My Lady!" a heart-wrenching call.
既有真心來問我　　　　"If you sincerely wish to test me,
亦唔該叫我做表兄身　　You should not address me as your cousin.
當初海誓山盟事　　　　We once vowed our love with the ocean and mountain
因何一旦盡拋沉　　　　　　as witnesses,
　　　　　　　　　　　Why did you throw all of that away in an instant?"
多嬌聽罷喉頭哽　　　　Hearing this, the lady sobs;
忍含淚珠便回音　　　　Holding back her tears, she replies,
既然你係梁公子　　　　"If you truly are Master Liang,
你把當年之事講奴聞　　Tell me what happened to us in those early days.
若是真情言不錯　　　　If what you say proves to be true,
等奴肺腑共談真　　　　Then I shall open my heart and we shall share our deepest thoughts."
亦滄聽罷如刀割　　　　Hearing her words, Liang feels a deep pain, as if being stabbed;
一聲長嘆淚交淋　　　　Heaving a deep sigh, his tears pour out.
不消提起當年事　　　　"It pains me to speak about those events in the past;
鐵石人聞亦碎心　　　　Even hearts of iron and stone would shatter at my tale.
當初姚府燈前會　　　　It began at the Yao family's Lantern Festival,

棋邊得會妹佳人
只為笑中傳語起
我估姑娘有我心
誰知拜壽歸家去
問跡尋蹤訪到上林
千金不惜就把書房買
起度橫門通過柳陰
只望四時同見面
唔想日日寒窗盼白雲
五經書史無心向
三飧茶飯幾時吞
為娘骨肉成枯槁
正係形容瘦損似條籐
初逢得見芸香面
採摘蘭花到柳陰
辭在亭前盡把相思訴
一一淒涼對妹陳
丫環見我多悲切
只話試娘心事有二分
自然不久傳音信
揖別歸房總未聞
小姐深閨如洞府
怎曉得我地漁人到問津

By the chess table I first made your acquaintance, my beautiful lady.
Your laughter gave hints of your feelings,
And I thought you had me in your heart.
Then I had to return home for a birthday party,
After which I searched for you, finally arriving in Shanglin County.
Without hesitation I spent a thousand gold pieces to buy a study next
    to your home;
Then I built a side-door that led to your garden through the willow
    trees.
I hoped that I could see you through all the seasons,
But all I saw were white clouds through my desolate window.
No longer interested in the Five Classics and other history books,
I even forgot to have my tea and three meals.
Because of you, my bones and flesh wasted away,
I became gaunt and could only be described as a rattan stick.
Then I met your maid Incense Fragrance
While she was picking orchids among the willow trees.
In front of the pavilion I told her how I longed for you,
Enumerating my sorrows in detail.
The maid understood my misery,
And said that she would find out her lady's feelings for me,
And that she would soon relay the news.
I bade farewell, returned to my room, and received no news;
Your secluded chamber was as quiet as a deep cave.
How could you know that I have been like the famous fisherman
    searching for Peach Blossom Village?

二次遊園嬌復遇
為著採蓮姐入柳陰
我早起垂楊花架下
嗰日逢嬌正斷魂
含愁盡把相思訴
衷情一一訴娘陳
望娘千萬同盟誓
猶如救活我雙親
嗰時姐不哀憐弟
好似絕了梁家拜孝墳
小姐堅心如鐵石
何曾瞅睬我半毫分
剛剛講到黃昏晚
姑娘拜別轉回行
主婢私談方過夜
對花長嘆五更深
有緣幸遇中秋節
小姐遊園看月輪
我在花間曾作揖
膝頭跪腫為佳人

Then when I wandered into the garden the second time, we met,
As you came to the willow grove to pick lotus blossoms in the pond.
I had risen early that day and was resting under the flower-covered
    trellis,
At the moment we met, I happened to be pining with misery.
With sorrow I described my lovesickness,
In great length I relayed to you in detail.
I asked you to swear an oath to me, to vow that you would marry me;
And if you did so, I would be as indebted to you as if you had saved
    the lives of my parents.
But you gave no pity to my pleading,
Making me feel as if my entire clan had died with no descendants to
    pay respect to the ancestral graves.
My lady, your resolute heart was as cold as iron and stone,
You paid me not a miniscule bit of attention.
I talked until nearly dusk,
When you bade me farewell and returned home.
You and your maids talked privately until dark,
But I spent the night sighing to the flowers until the fifth watch
    when dawn broke.
It must have been destined that we should meet again during the
    Mid-Autumn Festival,
When you came to enjoy the garden and admired the full moon.
I was in the midst of the flowers and greeted you with a bow,
Then I knelt in front of you until my knees were swollen, all for your
    sake.

銘感姑娘憐我苦
誓表真情花下盟
兩幅花箋為表記
妝台記得定唔曾
一心指望圖長遠
百歲歡娛冇乜改更
豈知發誓唔曾久
聞道天倫任滿轉回行
小弟柳陰曾哭別
嗰日分離劍刺心
歸家聽得爹爹講
姻緣許定姓劉人
我在芸窗身氣死
姑娘隔遠怎知因
後來用盡千般計
到底他鄉好習文
湊著雙親從我意
復往長洲見妹身
誰知入到園中去
單剩園公老邁人
話嬌隨任燕京去
我在看雲亭上氣死為佳人
感得園公將我救
又到姚弟窗前勸我習文

When you took pity on my suffering, how thankful I felt.
We vowed our true love in the garden amidst the flowers.
We wrote emblems of our love on two sheets of flowery parchment,
Don't you remember all that as you sat by your dressing table?
I had no other thoughts save for us to be together forever,
That our joy would last for a hundred years, a plan not to be changed.
Who could have known that soon after our vows,
I would receive news that my parents needed me so I returned home.
I bade you a tearful farewell in the willow grove,
My heart was pierced by a sword on the day we parted.
When I reached home my father informed me
That I had been betrothed to the daughter of a Liu family.
I almost died of anger right in my study,
How could you have known all that from afar?
I then tried every trick and scheme,
Eventually using the excuse of needing to study, I moved to another
    city.
Fortunately, my parents agreed,
So I returned to Changzhou to find you, my love.
But when I entered your family home,
I found only the elderly gardener there.
He told me that you had left for the Capitol with your parents.
I almost died of distress, there at the Cloudview Pavilion, at the
    thought of losing you.
I was grateful to the elderly gardener, who saved my life.
My cousin Yao advised me to concentrate on my studies.

帶病入場前去赴試
後來僥幸占高登
重在燕京城歇宿
翰苑重逢記得未曾
七尺泥牆吾亦跳過
只望同嬌結好親
後來聽得你爹邊外身遭困
小生唔望共成群
只話回朝去攬榜
斬卻胡人救你父親
嗰時兩美奇才事
安枕無憂結鳳群
誰想無能遭賊困
恐妨難得難離身
姐呀大抵姻緣二字潭中月
今生難望結成群

Eventually I sat for the imperial examination though I was ill,
But I was fortunate to succeed and received a high position.
I happened to be staying in the Capitol;
Do you not remember that we met again at the Imperial College?
I managed to jump over the seven-foot-high wall,
With the desire to marry you.
But then I heard the news that your father was trapped in battle
    under siege beyond the frontier,
I knew that I must postpone the hope of marrying you.
Instead I sought an appointment at the imperial court,
To go into battle, kill the barbarians, and save your father.
How wonderful, the double happiness of saving your father and
    marrying you,
Then I would be carefree and we would be reunited.
Who would have thought that, being inept, I would instead be
    trapped by the barbarians?
And fear that I would never return home alive.
My lady, our conjugal love is only as real as the moon reflected
    in the pond;
What hope is there for us to be united in this life?

華府領獎歌

人生世界上
東南西北是方向
落地喊三聲
好醜命生成
日月共同一個天
人生手足走路長
風流快活誰不想
人生何苦涯凄涼
千里遙遙別家鄉
來到美國十二年長
當初來時有咁想
三年兩載番吓家鄉
豈知天不從人樣
富貴貧窮命生成
生活問題嘅方向
全靠美國聯邦政府一力擔成
我雖文化水平淺
時時謹記在心前
今日來領獎
來到美國個京城
番心想一想
猶如舉子登科場

Fellowship Acceptance Song, Washington D.C.

We live in this world,
Whether east, south, west, or north.
Each baby as it is born cries three times,
And at that moment its fate for better or worse is sealed.
The sun and moon share the same sky,
We are born with hands and feet but the road we travel is long.
Who doesn't want to be carefree and happy?
Why would anyone want to suffer poverty and loneliness?
Leaving my hometown thousands of miles behind,
I came to the United States twelve long years ago.
When I first arrived I thought that
After two or three years I would return to my hometown.
But who would have thought that fate does not follow the
        wishes of men,
Wealth, honor, poverty, and obscurity are all pre-ordained.
But when it comes to questions of my livelihood,
I have completely relied on the U.S. government's strong hand.
Although I had little education,
I will always respectfully remember this.
Today I have come to accept my award,
Here in the capital of the United States.
As I ponder over this in my mind,
It is just as if I had passed the Chinese imperial examinations.

自古書中曾有講
姜公八十遇文王
我亦只估幾十歲人冇乜希望
誰知今日好似姜公遇文王
今日獲得美國國家藝術傳統獎
僥倖榜中有題名
我係中華民族來爭光
算來得獎也是光榮
今日來領獎
一邊唱時一邊領
歡天喜地笑洋洋
多謝列位官員主席步高陞
敬祝大家身壯力又健
人民富貴國家強
中美團結世界上
同心發展萬年長
我今唱歌仔
大家聽過時開運又開
四邊銀紙四邊來
老者聽過添福壽
男男女女聽過富貴榮華壽又長

Old books have said,
That Lord Jiang was already eighty before he met King Wen
　　　of the Zhou dynasty.
I also thought that a man with so many decades would have no future,
Who would have thought that today I am like Lord Jiang
　　　meeting King Wen?
Today I have won the American Master of Traditional Arts Award,
I am lucky to have my name appear amidst the awardees.
I have striven for this honor so as to represent the Chinese people,
But when you think about it, to receive this award is also a great
　　　personal triumph.
Today as I receive my award,
I receive it and sing of it at the same time.
With a joy that spreads over heaven and earth I am covered in smiles,
Repeated thanks to the chairperson and other officials, may you all
　　　advance in office.
I sincerely wish you all good health and vigor,
May the people be rich and the nation strong.
May China and America be united in this world,
And with one heart progress for ten thousand years.
I sing my little song today,
May all those who hear it have better and better luck.
May money come from all directions,
May the elderly in the audience live longer and happier lives,
May each man and each woman who hears this enjoy abundant
　　　wealth, prosperity, and longevity.

Uncle Ng and Family, 1993

Family gathering in August with his wife, children, spouses and grandchildren.

THE WHITE HOUSE

WASHINGTON

September 16, 1992

Dear Mr. Ng:

I am delighted to congratulate you on your recent
recognition by the National Endowment for the Arts.
The National Heritage Fellowship is awarded to a
select number of traditional American artists, and
you can be justifiably proud of this high honor.

Our Nation boasts a rich cultural heritage, and
through your fine work, you have not only helped
to preserve time-honored artistic traditions but
also added to the wealth of American folk art. The
United States is doubly enriched, as your talent,
skill, and dedication will undoubtedly inspire other
artists to follow in your quest for excellence,
thereby affirming the best in American art, history,
and culture.

Barbara joins me in sending best wishes to you for
continuing success.

Sincerely,

(signature: George Bush)

Mr. Ng Sheung-Chi
50 Norfolk Street
New York, New York 10002

The Folk Arts Program
of the National Endowment
for the Arts recognizes

Ng Sheung-Chi

As a Master Traditional Artist
who has contributed to
the shaping of our artistic
traditions and to preserving
the cultural diversity of
the United States

Chairman, National Endowment for the Arts

Director, Folk Arts Program

Chairman, National Heritage Fellowships Panel

[63]

Contributor Biographies

Robert Lee is the Co-Founder, Executive Director & Curator of the Asian American Arts Centre. Exhibiting contemporary artists for many years, he developed the Archive for Asian American artists embodying currently 1,600 artists from 1945 to the present. Artasiamerica.org—a digital reflection of this educational archive—makes accessible the beginnings of a history of an Asian American creative presence. Robert served for many years with The Association of American Cultures (TAAC) a national advocacy organization on diversity in the arts. He is the Executive Producer of the video "Singing to Remember."

Betty Lee Sung is Professor Emerita of the City College of New York. She has served as Chair of the Department of Asian Studies at City College of New York, and as Chair of the Board of Directors, Asian American/Asian Research Institute at CUNY. She is a pioneer in sparking the Asian American movement with her book, *Mountain of Gold: The Story of the Chinese in America* (1967) and subsequent articles and seven books.

Bell Yung, a professor of music at the University of Pittsburgh, is the recipient of numerous honors and fellowships including the Guggenheim, Mellon, Ford, ACLS, NEH, Fulbright, and Chiang Ching Kuo, and, in Hong Kong, from the Research Grants Council, Arts Development Council, Kwan Fong Foundation, and Bei Shan Tang Foundation. A specialist in the music of China, he has published ten books and over sixty scholarly articles, as well as a DVD, several CDs, and museum catalogues.

Eleanor S. Yung is a practitioner of Traditional Chinese Medicine and Acupuncture. She combines this with her teaching of Taichi at the Pacific College of Oriental Medicine, the Metropolitan Museum of Art, and classes in the West Village in New York City. Formerly, she was the Artistic Director of the Asian American Dance Theatre, and founder of the Asian American Arts Centre, serving on Advisory Panels of the National Endowment for the Arts, New York State Council on the Arts, and the Creative Artists Public Service Program.